# CATS

# SIAMESE CATS

## STUART A. KALLEN

ABDO & Daughters

Published by Abdo & Daughters, 4940 Viking Drive, Suite 622, Edina, Minnesota 55435.

Library bound edition distributed by Rockbottom Books, Pentagon Tower, P.O. Box 36036, Minneapolis, Minnesota 55435.

Printed in the United States.

Cover Photo credit: Firth Photo Bank
Interior Photo credits: Firth Photo Bank, page 11
Peter Arnold, Inc. pages 5, 19, 21

Photo Researchers, Inc. pages 9, 13, 15, 17


**Edited by Rosemary Wallner**


**Library of Congress Cataloging-in-Publication Data**


Kallen, Stuart A., 1955
        Siamese cat / by Stuart A. Kallen.
        p. cm. — (Cats)
Includes bibliographical references (p. 24) and index.
ISBN 1-56239-444-4
1. Siamese cat—Juvenile literature. [l. Siamese cat. 2. Cats.] I. Title. II. Series:
Kallen, Stuart A., 1955- Cats.
SF449.S5K35              1995
636.8'25--dc20

                                                        95-7579
                                                            CIP
                                                            AC

**ABOUT THE AUTHOR**
Stuart Kallen has written over 80 children's books,
including many environmental science books.

Second printing 2002

# Contents

# LIONS, TIGERS, AND CATS

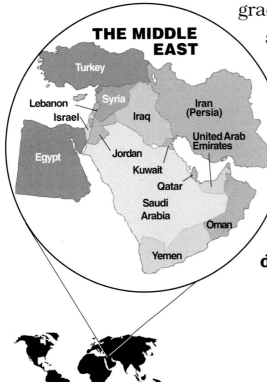

**THE MIDDLE EAST**

Turkey
Lebanon
Israel
Syria
Iraq
Iran (Persia)
Jordan
United Arab Emirates
Kuwait
Egypt
Qatar
Saudi Arabia
Oman
Yemen

Few animals are as beautiful and graceful as cats. And all cats are related. From the wild lions of Africa to the common house cat, all belong to the family **Felidae**. Cats are found almost everywhere. They include cheetahs, jaguars, lynx, ocelots, and the **domestic** cat.

People first **domesticated** cats around 5,000 years ago in the Middle East. Although humans have tamed them, house cats still think and act like their bigger cousins.

*All cats are related, from the cheetah to the domestic Siamese.*

# SIAMESE CATS

The country of Thailand was once known as Siam. It's impossible to say if Siamese cats really came from Siam. The **breed** was popular there, however. Wherever they came from, Siamese are one of the most popular and well-known cat breeds.

People first brought Siamese cats to England in 1884. The breed arrived in America a short time later. With their sleek coat and unusual looks, Siamese cats gained instant attention.

THAILAND

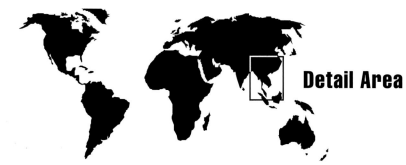

**Detail Area**

# WHAT THEY'RE LIKE

Siamese cats are proud, smart, and lovable. Most do not like strangers but will gladly curl up on their owner's lap. These cats have a loud voice. Their constant "talking" is hard to ignore.

*Siamese cats like to curl up in comfortable places.*

# COAT AND COLOR

There are four basic types of Siamese cats. Seal-**points** have cream coats with seal-brown markings. Blue-points have bluish-white coats with deep-blue markings. Chocolate-points have ivory coats with chocolate-brown markings. Lilac-points have off-white coats with frosty-gray markings. The fur on all Siamese cats is short, fine, and glossy. All Siamese cats have almond-shaped, slanted, bright blue eyes.

People have made new kinds of Siamese by **mating** this **breed** with other breeds. These new kinds are called colorpoint shorthairs.

*One type of Siamese cat is the blue-point.  It has a bluish-white coat with deep-blue markings.*

# SIZE

The Siamese is medium in size. Its body is long, slender, and noble. Its head is wedge-shaped with long and pointed ears. A Siamese's legs are long and thin. The paws are dainty, small, and oval.

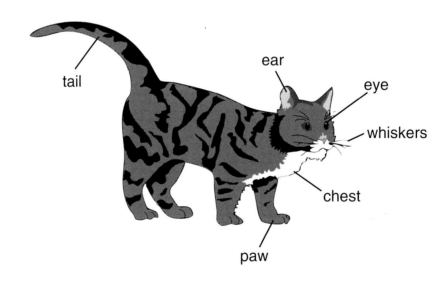

**Most cats share the same features.**

*The Siamese is a medium-size cat with a long body.*

# CARE

Like any pet, Siamese cats need much love and attention. Cats make fine pets. But they still have some of their wild **instincts**.

Cats are natural hunters and do well exploring outdoors. Giving them a scratching post where the cat can sharpen its claws saves furniture from damage.

Cats bury their waste and should be trained to use a litter box. The box needs to be cleaned every day.

Cats lick their coats to stay clean. A regular brushing will keep the cat from swallowing **hair balls** and becoming ill.

Cats love to play. A ball, **catnip**, or a loose string will keep a kitten busy for hours.

*Siamese cats need much love and attention.*

# FEEDING

Cats eat fish and meat. Hard bones that do not splinter help keep the cat's teeth and mouth clean. Water should always be available. Most cats enjoy dried cat food. Kittens drink their mother's milk. However, milk can cause illness in adult cats.

*Siamese cats need a well-balanced diet to stay happy and healthy.*

# KITTENS

Female cats are **pregnant** for about sixty-five days. Litters range from two to eight kittens. The average cat has four kittens.

Kittens are blind and helpless for the first several weeks. About three weeks later, they will start crawling and playing. At this time they may be given cat food. Nearly a month later, kittens will run, wrestle, and play games.

If the cat is a **pedigree**, it should be registered and given papers at this time. At ten weeks the kittens are old enough to be sold or given away.

*Female cats are pregnant for about sixty-five days.*
*Litters range from two to eight kittens.*

# BUYING A KITTEN

The best place to get a Siamese cat is from a **breeder**. Cat shows are also good places to find kittens.

You must decide if you want a simple pet or a show winner. A basic Siamese can cost $50. Blue-ribbon winners can cost as much as $1,000. When you buy a Siamese, get **pedigree** papers that register the animal with the Cat Fanciers Association.

When buying a kitten, check it closely for signs of good health. The ears, nose, mouth, and fur should be clean. Eyes should be bright and clear. The cat should be alert and interested in its surroundings. A healthy kitten will move around with its head held high.

*Kittens should have bright, clear eyes.*

# GLOSSARY

**BREED** - To raise or grow; also a group of animals that look alike and have the same type of ancestors.

**BREEDER** - A person who breeds animals or plants.

**CALICO** (KAL-ih-koe) - A cat that is black, red, cream, and white in color.

**CATNIP** - A strong-smelling plant used as stuffing for cat toys.

**DOMESTICATE** (doe-MESS-tih-kate) - Tamed or adapted to homelife.

**FELIDAE** (FEE-lih-day) - Latin name given to the cat family.

**GROOMING** - Cleaning.

**HAIR BALLS** - Balls of fur that gather in a cat's stomach after grooming itself by licking.

**INSTINCT** - A way of acting that is born in an animal, not learned.

**MATE** - To join in a pair in order to produce young.

**PEDIGREE** (PED-ih-gree) - A record of an animal's ancestors.

**POINTS** - The markings on an animal's legs, head, and tail.

**PREGNANT** - With one or more babies growing inside the body.

**TABBY** - A cat with striped fur.

# Index

# BIBLIOGRAPHY

Alderton, David. *Cats.* New York: Dorling Kindersley, 1992.

Clutton-Brock, Juliet. *Cat.* New York: Alfred A. Knopf, 1991.

Denlinger, Milo. *The Complete Siamese Cat.* New York: Howell Book House, 1978.

Taylor, David. *The Ultimate Cat Book.* New York: Simon & Schuster, 1989.